Tap it

Sam taps.
Tap, tap, tap.

Sam did it.

Dan taps it.
Tap, tap, tap.

Dan did it.

Tap, tap, tap.

Dan and Sam did it.

Pam is in it.

Tap it   Level 1: Story 4

Before reading

Say the sounds: s a t p i n m d

Practise blending the sounds: tap Dan Pam Sam taps

High-frequency words: it in and did Dad   **Tricky words:** I is

Vocabulary check: tap – What does it mean when you "tap" something? (Demonstrate tapping your finger against a surface). If you used a hammer, what would you tap with it? The word "tap" in this case is a verb (action word). What does the word "tap" refer to as a noun (thing)?

Story discussion: Look at the cover. What does it look like the children might be doing?

Teaching points: Talk about the use of commas to show small pauses and to separate words in a list. Talk about full stops to show the end of a sentence. Review the use of speech bubbles to show what a character is saying.

After reading

Comprehension:
- What did the boys build?
- What did the boys use to make the house?
- Who was the house for?
- Do you think Pam liked it? How do you know?

Fluency: Speed read the words again from the inside front cover.